what's your excuse
for not
overcoming stress

what's your excuse ...

FOR NOT

OVERCOMING STRESS?

Overcome your excuses for less stress and more control, calm and resilience

kelly swingler

"An easy, stress-free read! Kelly's pragmatic and non-judgmental approach shines through and if you are serious about transforming the stress levels in your life she provides simple and practical solutions for you to try. We're all different with different pressures but it feels like there's something for everyone in here"

Jackie Perkins, director of House of Colour

"Great book, packed with really useful, practical tips. As a busy working mum there are many hints and tips that I will take away and apply. Kelly writes in an easy, friendly way which makes it simple to read and to find the sections most relevant to you. Love it!"

Claudia Bangs, HR director

"This book gives an insight into how our thoughts cause stress reactions that can get quickly out of control and provides helpful tools to deal with things in our everyday life. Great read, highly recommended"

Jody Kay, Sound and Movement

"A really useful book to have to hand. It's like having someone around to smooth your brow and hold your hand whilst quietly reminding you how to stop stress taking over! Great ideas – you need this in your desk drawer!"

Jo Thresher, author and director of Better with Money

"A practical, user-friendly book packed with tips, techniques and real life scenarios which will resonate in one way or another with you or with someone you know. Too busy, too stressed, too much? This book will help you to begin the inner work, make the changes and see the differences which only you can take charge of. Make the change"

Jane Tribaudi, HR consultant

"Really highlights the areas of life which raise normal levels of stress to unmanageable levels and which leave so many of us with feelings of overwhelm, anxiety and distress. Kelly not only explains why you feel this way but gives you the actions you can take to reduce and manage the stressful situations you face. If you feel stressed or unable to cope with the pressures in your life then this book is a great resource"

Gary Johannes, founder of Inspired to Change and senior lecturer at Clifton Practice Hypnotherapy Training

"Kelly is able to take complex ideas and simplify them and in this book applies that approach to the subject of stress. We can all let things get out of control and feel stress in our lives but the tools in this book will help to you to overcome these and to stop making excuses"

Michael Fearnhead, managing director of Chrysalis Consultingb

Also in this series

What's Your Excuse for not Overcoming Stress?

This first edition published in 2017 by WYE Publishing
9 Evelyn Gardens, Richmond TW9 2PL
www.wyepublishing.com

ISBN 978-0-9956052-6-8

Cover and text design by Annette Peppis & Associates

'What's Your Excuse…?' is a UK Registered Trade Mark
(Registration No: 3018995)

www.whatsyourexcuse.co.uk
Follow What's Your Excuse…? on Twitter – @whats_yr_excuse
www.facebook.com/whatsyourexcusebooks

http://www.chrysalis-consulting.co.uk/
Follow Kelly on Twitter – @kelly_swingler

Contents

Introduction

How this book will help you

You've got a lot going on in your life. You're always busy, always rushing around and always trying to squeeze in one more thing. You never have any time for yourself and find yourself wondering how you will ever get everything done. Your stress levels are at a constant high. And when you talk about how stressed you are with your family, friends or colleagues they respond by telling you just how stressed they are too.

We rarely give ourselves time to switch off anymore, to just sit or sleep or simply *be*. It's become normal to be constantly busy and stressed.

Technology can make life easier, but constant phone calls, emails, news feeds, notifications and messages often make it harder instead. And if you do find a few minutes to relax you could well be interrupted so that your stress levels rise before they've even had a chance to fall.

But it doesn't have to be like this.

I am a coach, hypnotherapist and psychotherapist and I have helped many people to overcome and reduce stress in their lives. After years of research and study I understand the causes of stress and its impact and I know from my own experiences the benefits of learning to manage and reduce your own stress levels.

It *is* possible to take control of your life to reduce stress to a healthy level and in this book I will tell you how to do it.

What is stress?

Stress in itself is not a bad thing. In fact a little stress is good for us. Yes that's right, some stress is good for us, as long as it's maintained at a healthy level.

Stress is what helped primitive humans stay safe. It's what has helped the human race survive and evolve. It's what makes us innovative, it helps us to get out of bed in the morning and it makes us feel alive.

Healthy levels of stress keep us motivated in our work, drive us to improve our time when we go running, help us to plan events, move house, get married, apply for a promotion at work or start our own business.

But stress becomes harmful when it goes beyond those helpful levels and at that point it impacts our health and wellbeing.

The consequences of too much stress include:

- Disrupted sleep patterns
- Poor food choices
- Damage to our relationships
- Poor performance at work
- Brain fog, where you struggle to communicate or think clearly
- Withdrawal from the fun things in life
- Feelings of agitation

- Feelings of overwhelm
- Poor physical health

So it's really important for your own wellbeing and happiness that you take control of your stress levels.

The good news

In the past when I experienced high levels of stress I would seek advice on how to reduce it, but then I struggled to put any recommendations into practice because I always had excuses to explain why I was so stressed and why I couldn't take action to change things.

The good news is that when I started to listen to and address my excuses I started to feel more in control, and was able to take practical steps towards a better, calmer, happier life.

Listen to your own reasons (excuses) for being stressed. They will give you an indication of what you most need to change.

In this book I take a look at all of the excuses I've heard from clients to explain why they've tolerated unhealthy levels of stress. Some of the excuses may read like a chapter of your own life, others may not resonate as much, but in this book I hope to help you to identify where and why you are creating or tolerating stress in your own life and I'll offer advice, ideas and inspiration to help you overcome it.

When you do, this is what you can expect:

- Increased energy
- Clearer thinking
- Healthier and happier relationships
- Increased performance in all areas of your life
- Better sleeping patterns
- Less forgetfulness
- More enthusiasm for healthy eating and exercise
- Increased feelings of control over the events in your life
- Increased resilience
- Feelings of calmness
- A desire to look forward to the future and let go of the past
- More focus and drive
- Improved overall health
- A desire to get back to the things you love in life

It *is* possible to lead a life which is not dominated by stress and that life will be a happier, healthier one.

The Excuses

Beliefs

I worry too much

I'll let you into a secret. It's not the events in our lives which cause stress but our own reactions to them and how we think about them, rather than the events themselves.

If we have a negative thought it's converted into anxiety and one of the most common ways we create anxiety is by negatively forecasting the future; for instance believing that you'll be single for the rest of your life or that you'll lose your job. Things which *haven't actually happened yet.*

If we have a negative thought it's converted into anxiety

Our minds can't tell the difference between imagination and reality. To try this out close your eyes, take a couple of deep breaths and imagine you are in your kitchen at home. On the worktop in front of you is a bowl of bright yellow lemons. You pick one up, hold it to your nose and breathe in the lemony scent. You place the lemon on the worktop next to you, grab a knife and chopping board and start to slice the lemon.

Think about putting a slice in your mouth.

I can't do that exercise without a tension in my jaw from the sourness of the lemon. Thinking about a situation can cause your body to react as if that situation is actually happening.

It's the same with worry and stress. If you believe things are going to go badly you'll create stress which will be just as real as if those things were actually happening.

In order to reduce the worrying you'll need to address your negative thought patterns. There's no point in worrying about things which haven't happened yet, and worrying won't stop them happening anyway! Now you might think changing thought patterns sounds difficult, and at first it may be challenging, but with time and practice it can be done.

Becoming more aware is the first step. Each time you catch yourself thinking or speaking negatively about the future ask yourself why you are doing this.

Also, when you find yourself thinking negatively about things which *might* happen, ask yourself what's the worst that *can* happen, and I mean the worst possible scenario. In some cases it won't actually be that bad, and in other cases it will be so far-fetched you might well realise it's pretty unlikely. Then take time to consider the best case scenario too.

When I first started my company I was asked to

speak at an event, something I had always done and always loved, but never just as *me*; I had previously always been speaking as a representative of a big, respected brand. I got myself so stressed about it on the journey to the event that I was tempted to turn the car round, go home and make an excuse such as illness so I that I didn't have to attend. Instead, I considered the worst case – messing up what I was going to say – which actually wasn't *that* bad, and the best case, which included new clients, a milestone speaking event as me, increased confidence and potential new speaking opportunities. I continued my journey, delivered my presentation, got some amazing feedback and two new clients.

Be aware of what is triggering your own anxiety about certain situations, take time to consider the best and worst outcomes, and you'll start to take a more realistic, positive view of the future. Over time the old negative thought patterns should happen less and less.

Now, if you're worrying about something over which you have control, then take control and change it.

For instance, as a business owner I can spend time worrying about where my next client is coming from or I can take action to find that client. And if what I do doesn't work then I'll need to try a different approach.

Worrying about my weight is also no good for me. If I'm not happy with my weight I am better off directing my energy into making better food choices and doing some exercise than I am worrying about how I look.

Take action to change what you can change.

Finally, every negative thought we do have is accumulated and stored. I call this storage place our stress bucket. Thankfully, we do have a method for emptying this bucket: the phase of sleep known as rapid eye movement – REM. During this type of sleep we re-run events of the day and change them from emotional memories to narrative memories. Memories we have control over.

> Take action to change what you can change

For instance, someone upsets you one afternoon and you are still thinking about it when you go to bed. When you wake in the morning you might well have forgotten about the incident, or if you haven't you will at least feel better about it. Remember the saying 'I'll sleep on it'? That relates to the therapeutic benefit of sleep.

If you need to improve the quality of your sleep here are some things to try:

- Switch off your phone, laptop and tablet at least two hours before bed
- Don't watch anything on TV before bed that will increase your adrenalin such as crime dramas or action films

- Avoid caffeine, sugar or any other stimulants at least two hours before bed
- Write down your thoughts and feelings in a journal to clear your head of the day's events
- Before you go to sleep take five deep breaths: in through your nose and out through your mouth

I like to think that I wake up every morning with my stress bucket emptied so that I can start the new day without stress, anxiety, anger, depression or fear and you can too if you get regular, good quality sleep.

I've always been the family worrier

Who gave you this label, and why do you hang on to it?

A client of mine was a 'worrier'. She worried about work, home life, health, difficult conversations, following her dreams, being different, doing what she really wanted, saying no, upsetting people, not being good enough and so on and so on. She worried about *everything*.

During our first coaching session it became clear that worrying is what her entire family had been telling her she did since she was two years old. She was told she was a worrier, so she learnt to worry. We explored how it might feel to not worry, and worked out a plan for her to reframe her experiences with more positive thoughts so that instead of worrying she would adopt a carefree approach, even if only for an hour. I asked her to say, 'I am carefree' out loud a few times.

When she did this the changes in her body language and in her posture were instant. Her shoulders lowered, her face lit up, the tension fell from her jaw, her eyes shone and she smiled.

I asked how this felt and she said it was wonderful. She laughed and said that her family would think she had lost the plot but that she was determined to try it out at her sister's hen party which was coming up. She'd been worrying about it for weeks and was worried that her mood would ruin the weekend for her sister, particularly as she was worrying about the other bridesmaids as well.

If you always label yourself as 'stressed' you'll always be stressed

I got an email from her the following week. Her new carefree approach had allowed her to make a decision about working abroad for a few months, something she had always wanted to do. Later, she described the hen party as 'amazing', said that she was enjoying her job more, was getting more involved in meetings and that her performance at work was improving and that she felt 'amazing'. She still had times of worry, but it was no longer all-consuming or suffocating her in the way it had previously.

She no longer considered herself a worrier, she was carefree.

And that's the thing with labels. If you always label yourself as 'stressed' you'll always *be* stressed and if you act out the labels applied to you by other people that's how they will always see you and how you will continue to act around them.

Take a look at the Three Ps at the end of this book which will help you to readjust your beliefs, to free yourself from labels or to create new and positive ones for yourself.

Then, think of the words you use to describe how you react to difficult situations and replace them with something more positive. How does that feel?

I can't remember when I didn't feel stressed

Really? Were you stressed as soon as you opened your eyes this morning? Were you stressed in the shower? Were you stressed when you closed the front door? Or when you were singing along to the radio in the car this morning? Are you stressed right now as you sit reading this book?

If you have just answered yes to all of these, try to think of just a minute or two from this morning or last night where you weren't stressed, just one or two minutes. What was different at that time that made you feel calmer?

I like to use smokers as an example of how we misrepresent how much of our time is taken up with certain feelings. Let's say that on average a smoker smokes twenty cigarettes per day and that each cigarette takes two minutes to smoke. In total, that's forty minutes in a day when they are actually a smoker and twenty-three hours and twenty minutes of every day when they aren't. Yet a smoker will tell you they can't get through anything without smoking.

So can you honestly, hand on heart, without a shadow of a doubt, say that you are stressed twenty-four hours a day, seven days a week?

Try this: take a piece of paper and draw a line. Mark the twenty-four hours of the day along it. Put a blue circle around the hours that you feel calm and a red circle around the hours that you feel stressed.

You might be surprised at just how few hours you are stressed

You might be surprised at just how few hours you *are* stressed, but you just haven't been noticing the time when you are calm.

Now, look at the hours you've circled in red and consider what you can do to reduce the stress during those hours so that you don't feel overwhelmed by it. This could be taking a break and going for a walk, writing down how you are feeling, grabbing a green tea instead of yet another coffee, scheduling ten minutes of calm in between meetings, blocking out one day a week where you have no meetings so that you can focus on other tasks, washing up (sounds dull but it can help us feel instantly grounded and calm – I have no idea why), having a bath, going for a run, having lunch with a friend. Anything which relieves the pressure or gives you a break from it.

Then focus on the hours you've circled in blue: times when you feel calm, in control or whatever feeling or word you associate with those better times. Identify why you don't feel stress at these times and do more of it.

You might find it helpful to repeat this exercise regularly over the next few weeks to give you a broader picture, and to keep you focused on making some changes to your routine and to your perception of how much stress you actually have in your life.

I'm a procrastinator

You've got loads to do, you know you have a deadline, but you spend hours on social media, you do housework or other lower priority chores, you turn on the TV, make a drink, walk the dog – anything but the tasks you really should be doing!

You don't know where or how to start and it's stressful. And then you find your stress increasing because you're going to miss your deadline, or it feels too hard, but you still can't bring yourself to take action to get anything done because it all just feels too overwhelming.

Take a piece of paper and write down all of the things you think you should be doing. Cross off anything that isn't important today, and see what's left. Pick one task and start it.

You could just set a timer for just fifteen minutes. Start it and see how you get on. Step away from social media or whatever else it is that you are using as a distraction and make a start. What is fifteen minutes anyway? You've probably wasted far more time than that already!

Also, consider these other potential reasons for your procrastination:

- Are you holding back through fear, not necessarily

of failure but of success – what will happen if you actually achieve this?

* Or is the answer to 'what's in it for me?' not a big enough driving factor for you? It's just not hitting the right buttons for you

Get to the bottom of what's causing your procrastination and you may just solve the problem, reducing the related feelings of stress when you start making progress.

Isn't stress just normal these days?

I hear this a lot, and yes, unfortunately it does appear to be the new normal.

When something becomes a habit we start to notice it less and less and it just becomes part of our normal experience.

But stress doesn't *have* to be normal. You don't have to put up with this feeling or get used to it if it is making you unhappy.

If you work out why you feel stressed and which areas of your life make you feel stressed you can take action to change your behaviour and your reactions.

For instance, a friend of mine was experiencing issues

with high blood pressure and she was asked to monitor it. Through this she realised that it was higher on the days she worked but not while she was in the office. She enjoyed her work but got stressed on the journey to and from work. It wasn't the job, it was the journey. She changed to a route which took a little longer but it was less stressful and she started to enjoy the journey more. Her blood pressure reduced because of this.

Can you pinpoint the times when your stress levels are at their highest, or the situations in which you feel most unhappy by monitoring your body's responses? Perhaps you feel a flutter in your stomach, your shoulders might tense, you might grind your jaw, crack your knuckles, reach for food, sleep more, sleep less, shout at people or withdraw. Use these to identify the things you most need to change and then use the advice in the appropriate chapters of this book to tackle them.

Stress doesn't have to be your normal.

Stress doesn't bother me

This may sound a little odd, but some people subconsciously *like* stress. I've met people over the years who like being known as difficult, stressed or miserable, because by acting in this way they avoid certain people and situations.

Are you secretly enjoying the feeling of stress because it's helping you to avoid changing something that needs changing, or doing something new? Starting a diet, joining a gym or looking for a new job?

Be honest with yourself.

I hate delegating

For a long period of time I was a control freak who dared not delegate to anyone because I believed they wouldn't be able to do it my way, and it would be quicker to do it myself than have to teach someone else to do it. The fact that I was stressed because I had too much to do and that delegating to someone else would have solved the problem in the longer term completely escaped me. I was stuck in my world of stress trying to do everything my way.

It's true that nobody will do things your way, because it's *your* way. But they can do it *their* way, and their way might be just as good (or even better) than yours. And yes, it will take you time in the short-term to train someone else on what needs to be done but long-term it can save you time, energy and stress.

Also, think about why you don't want to hand over a task. Are you secretly enjoying complaining about being stressed, enjoying being a martyr or putting yourself on a pedestal where everyone thinks you are amazing for being able to take on so much and do everything so well (when really you're a swan: cool on the outside but paddling frantically underneath)?

You probably delegate lots of things in your life already. Does someone else cook dinner at home sometimes? Does someone else drive you round at the weekends? Do you have a cleaner, a gardener, a childminder, a babysitter or an assistant at the office?

Start delegating more and you'll find that you have more time to do the tasks you're best suited to doing, thereby increasing your performance and levels of satisfaction. It also helps others to try new things, to develop their skills and to grow in confidence.

You probably delegate lots of things in your life already

Stress motivates me

Stress can be a good motivator, if it's at the right level and at the right time.

Sports people thrive on stress. Adrenaline keeps them competitive. But there will come a time when they can longer maintain this and they retire due to injury or illness. Stress can be a good motivator, but it's not sustainable long-term.

A few years ago I was involved in a large project at work. After many years of long hours and work pressures my body was telling me to slow down. I ignored it. I kept on going, kept on pushing and kept on working. Eventually I could go on no more, and because I had ignored the small but regular stress signals that my body had been presenting me with for months, I found myself suddenly out of action for almost seven months.

I vowed never to let myself to get to that point again. I re-prioritised my life and I've learned to listen to my body.

So you may well be enjoying a certain level of stress now, but watch out for warning signs and *listen to them*. Don't let stress accumulate unnoticed as I did. If you learn how to recognise when motivational healthy stress is being taken over by unhealthy stress you'll be in a good place to keep it under control.

Signs of unhealthy stress are:

- Headaches
- Lethargy
- Loss of interest in things

- Decreased performance
- Aches and pains
- Frequent minor illnesses
- Forgetfulness
- Irritability
- Feelings of overwhelm
- Brain fog

Learn to listen to your body, pay attention to warning signs and if necessary take action. Be proactive and schedule some regular rest time so that your body gets a chance to slow down a little and not reach the crash and burn stage.

Work

I have a stressful job

Can you identify which part of the job is stressful? Is your workload overwhelming, are your colleagues not pulling their weight or is your manager driving you insane? Are you being bullied, suffering from budget cuts or overly demanding customers?

If you can identify what or who is causing your stress, you can focus on tackling that particular problem. You can have conversations with your manager or another colleague about how you are feeling. You can opt for reduced hours. You can say no to certain tasks where your workload is already too much or where you feel there is no value added. You can help other people understand and respect your workload and your priorities. You can help other people prioritise their own workloads so they don't present you with work which has suddenly become urgent. You can delegate more.

You do not have to be all things to all people nor do you have to do everything you are asked.

On top of this, the concept of work/life balance can be a difficult thing to achieve, and yet so many of us see it as the holy grail of a happy life. Why? There are 168 hours in a week. Let's say you work 40 hours per week, which would leave you with 128 hours. Take away 7 hours' sleep each night and you're down to just 79 hours in the week in which you have to commute, eat, socialise, exercise, rest, spend time with your family and do anything else you enjoy.

When you look at it that way it seems quite depressing, but it's the reason why seeking work/life balance in your life can make you feel stressed, so you need to look at it from a new perspective. I like to talk about life balance or life alignment which is about living with purpose, achieving your goals and feeling how you want to feel.

So focus on how you want to feel at the end of the working week and work towards that. Do you want to feel successful? Rested? Energised? Motivated? Happy? Then adjust the way you use your time and go about your work accordingly.

A 'to-be' list can be much more effective than a 'to-do' list.

I'm always first in and last out

There's a common misconception in the workplace that working long hours is a sign of commitment, but it's a misconception we need to fix. Rushing to be the first one in the office in the morning and staying to be the last one out in the evening is not productive, it's not helpful and you aren't doing yourself any favours.

When was the last time you had a productive day at work? Not a busy or long day, but a *productive* one.

Try starting your working day not by thinking about how busy you are going to be or how much you have to get done, but by thinking about how productive and effective you can be. It's not about sitting at your desk from dawn to dusk just to show you are present. I've dismissed people for being at their desk all hours of the day, but not actually doing any work. (This in itself would make me stressed, how on earth can you pretend to be busy all day and get nothing done?!)

Don't believe that spending long days in the office makes you look competent or valuable; it can often give the opposite impression. Work well within your official hours and establish a better work/ life balance. Your relationships, health and social life will all benefit from it.

You might also find "I wouldn't want anyone to think I'm lazy" helpful.

I can't choose how I spend my time at work

Unless you are being micro-managed by your boss (and if you are maybe it's time for a chat with them or to start looking for a new job), then you probably do have some say in how you manage your time at work.

So many people want their boss to treat them like adults rather than children but fail to act in a mature, responsible, adult way. Your boss may appreciate it if you ask to set and review your own objectives, so don't wait for them to make the call or arrange the meeting.

And even if you have set tasks for the day, you can still manage certain stressors. Split your day into ninety minute blocks and ideally, unless it's your core job, only check your emails first thing in the morning, at midday and at the end of the day. Then use the rest of the day to focus on what you need to get done.

If your boss hasn't given you a breakdown of what you need to be doing every minute of every day you *do* have control of your working day and you *can* choose to make it as effective as possible to reduce your stress levels.

Focus on productive instead of busy

Prioritise, don't procrastinate and focus on productive instead of busy. You can do this by thinking of all that you need to achieve on a certain day, combining this with how you want to feel. Ever growing to-do lists can overwhelm you. I find that the most useful way of managing a to-do list is to schedule the time directly into your diary instead of just listing all of the things that will keep you busy.

Once you put this into practice you'll find that you perform to a higher standard, achieve more, feel better about yourself and feel calmer and more in control.

I have a horrible commute

How are you commuting? Is there a different way to travel? Could you get the train instead of driving? Could you car-share? Could you work from home sometimes?

I used to spend three hours a day on a train to and from work plus time on a tube train and a drive to and from the station. I resented this, until I realised that I could use the time on the train more wisely, to help myself and to reduce stress. Some days I worked on the train which resulted in fewer hours in the office; some days I listened to music, read, meditated, researched my next holiday or indulged in online shopping. My commute became a more positive, productive time and no longer something I resented.

If you take a train, take some time to think about how you could change your own travelling experience.

Think about how you could change your own travelling experience

If you drive you can also find ways to enjoy the journey. Put on your favourite feel-good music, listen to an audio book or simply take time to enjoy the solitude and gather your thoughts. If you regularly get stuck in traffic, leave earlier or later to avoid the busiest times, and if you struggle to find a parking space at your destination park further away and enjoy a short walk in the time you'd usually be driving round and round looking for a space.

A calmer, more pleasant journey will mean that you arrive at your destination feeling calmer and more positive and this is likely to result in a calmer, more productive, more positive day.

I can't switch off, even on holiday

You need your holiday, you've been waiting for it and looking forward to it for so long but as the time approaches you become stressed about everything you have to do before you go.

You have three choices:

- Work extra hard in the run up to your holiday
- Do what you can and work whilst you are away
- Do what you can, delegate the rest or leave it until you get back

Most people I know opt for one of the first two options, neither of which do them any good, and both of which prevent them from properly benefiting from their long-awaited break. If you don't switch off and recharge while you're away you'll become even more stressed when you get back.

Interestingly, in addition to this, many of us come back from holidays in desperate need of another one because we haven't rested properly while we were away. We often have to wake up and travel to and from our destination at strange hours of the day or night, we pack in too many activities, overindulge with food and alcohol and party until the early hours of the morning.

I've covered the importance of good quality sleep in "I worry too much" but it's important even when you're on holiday. Alcohol, caffeine, chocolate, sugar and other stimulants reduce the amount of quality sleep we're able to get in a night and when we are away we tend to have more of these things.

The less sleep we have, the less we are able to

empty our stress bucket; the less we empty our bucket the more stressed we get. So we can return from our holiday feeling worse than before we left and if you work while you're away you're never recharging in the way that you should be.

Give yourself a proper break

So don't work or think about work while you're on holiday. Give yourself a proper break and when you get back to the office you'll be in a better position to handle the workload you left behind. Set your out-of-office with a message that says you have no access to your emails until the day after your return (this also gives you a day to get on top of your emails before more pile in) and switch off emails on your phone whilst you're away. Don't answer calls that you know are work related. Keep your diary clear for your first half day or full day back in the office. Don't try to reply to all of the emails that have been received; instead arrange calls or meetings with the people who have sent the most emails for a more efficient update on all of the matters. Stay in control.

Returning to work fully refreshed and recharged will mean you are much better able to deal with the work you'll be returning to, and you'll deal with it in a calmer manner, meaning less stress after your holiday too.

Family

I have to look after my family

Being a parent or carer brings a lot of responsibility but it doesn't have to be stressful. It is a challenge to change your thoughts, reactions and priorities in order to reduce the stress related to this responsibility but it can be done, even if it has to be done gradually.

At twenty-four I was a single mum, money was really tight and I had to sell my car to make ends meet. I had to walk my boys to nursery and walk to work which took up more of my precious time. Trying to fit everything in was making me very unhappy, but I broke everything down into tasks, created a routine for myself and stuck to it. Things started to get easier. Not because I had less to do, but because I felt more in control. Getting organised is key to reducing the stress. Take a look at the tips in the chapter on organisation later in this book.

As a parent or carer you may not be getting enough good quality sleep, and that will impact your stress levels and make it even harder to cope. When we are deciding how to spend our time sleep often comes way down the list of priorities, but sleep is important and if you don't get enough you'll struggle to stay on top of everything you have to do, which may cause you more stress and make it harder to sleep: a vicious cycle.

So weigh up what's most important: sleep or social media, sleep or that last email, sleep or the latest episode of your favourite programme, sleep or housework. Get enough sleep and you'll feel more positive, more energetic and more able to get things done. It's a win-win.

Get enough sleep and you'll feel more positive

See more about getting more sleep in "I worry too much".

Isn't stress normal if you're a parent?

As I mentioned in the introduction, a healthy amount of stress is good for us and indeed entirely normal, but it's your thoughts relating to events which cause stress, not the events themselves.

Just thinking about the chaos at breakfast, trying to get the kids dressed, doing the school run and drop off, driving to work, receiving the phone call from school about the forgotten PE kit and the last minute rush to get out of the office and home before the after school activities finish can feel stressful if you see these things as something extra that you have to do on top of everything else in your life. However the reality is that this *is* your life.

Think back to school or university and how you struggled to fit everything in then on top of your lessons and lectures. Then you found yourself at work with longer hours and more responsibility plus new tasks such as looking after your house, cooking for yourself, etc.

Life changes and responsibilities and tasks change with it. Change your perception of these

Change your perception of these 'new' family responsibilities

'new' family responsibilities and accept that they are part of who you are now.

If you have babies or young children it's likely that you're not getting enough sleep, and as I've mention already, a lack of sleep prevents us from emptying our stress bucket and leaves us open to building up more stress over time. So take a look at "I worry too much" and "I have to look after my family" for more on getting good quality sleep.

Sleep when you can and make sleep a priority. Who

cares about the pile of washing and the fact you haven't washed your hair in a week? Do what you can when you can.

Incidentally, I know some parents with three or four young children who cope extremely well and are some of the calmest people you will ever meet but I also know parents of one baby who are so stressed I'm amazed they are functioning at all. A health visitor explained to me that first time mums worry and panic more than mums of three or four children. As a first time parent you worry about whether you are doing the right thing for your baby, whether the noise is normal, whether their cry means there is something wrong, whether they are sleeping properly and eating properly and whether you are a good mum or not. If you're a first time parent it's worth noting this.

I'm neglecting my relationships

I recently read about a woman who had decided to leave her job. She said that whilst she loved her job she realised that she had been living to work. She had put work first and missed what turned out to be her grandmother's last birthday. She had cancelled social events with family and friends, she had let her health suffer and she let her marriage break down because she had prioritised her job.

I can identify with this. I always felt so proud of myself for progressing my career so quickly whilst being there for my parents when they were ill and attending sports days and parents' evenings for my sons. But in reality I was missing the important things. I was missing the conversations on the way to school, shared meals, bath time, bed time and the stories about their day at school and what they had achieved.

I was missing quality time with my husband talking about his day, my day and our relationship. My marriage ultimately broke down, because of our differences, friendships drifted apart, and my health started to suffer because I let my job get in the way. But I was so busy at the time I didn't see what was happening.

Now, since starting my own business, my relationships come first. I can look carefully at how many mornings a week I'm out of the house early and how many nights a week I'm back late or out at meetings. I don't always get it right, but I am more attentive to all of my relationships, even though I have to keep an eye on it and reposition and re-prioritise constantly.

My partner and I have a 'date night' once a week. We work around when the kids are out or away, when we don't have to be somewhere for work and we schedule it in our diaries. It's not always something super glamorous or expensive. Sometimes it's a three course meal at a lovely restaurant but more often it's a walk around the lake with the dog, a walk to the local pub, a takeaway, a film night or sometimes it's tidying the house together. What's important isn't what we do, it's that we do it together. But we have to prioritise it or else it won't happen, because there are always other things to do.

It can be done. Take action and do something before it's too late. Agree a date night, have a family only day in your diary once a month (if not every week), schedule a night out that is just for you and friends, book time with your wider family. Put those things in your diary well in advance before your diary gets filled up and start to enjoy happier relationships again.

Other People

Everyone expects so much from me

Have you allowed yourself to get into a pattern of saying yes to everyone and become a people pleaser?

It can be hard not to say yes. Your kids, parents, partner, colleagues have all come to rely on you, you've always delivered, always been the strong one, the shoulder to cry on or the top performer.

You'd feel guilty if you changed the way you deal with things, so you keep on going, tolerating more pressure and stress in your own life because you don't want to make things difficult for anyone else.

Behaviour breeds behaviour and if you've never set boundaries, said no, pushed back or explained how much pressure you're being put under then you're never going to break the cycle.

Set some boundaries for yourself about what you will and won't do

Your ongoing kindness and support may have created a belief in others that you will always be there for them.

How can you change that? Practise saying no. Set some boundaries for yourself about what you will and won't do. Offer an alternative or suggest someone else who may be of help instead. Don't feel like you have to let things continue as they are.

See also "I find it hard to say no to people".

I find meeting new people difficult

I used to hate meeting new people, not because I don't like people, but because I'm an introvert and was quite shy so preferred to keep a close circle of people around me. New groups of people terrified me. This is something that was with me from childhood, through school and into the workplace.

I used to dread big family gatherings, large meetings or networking events. I've never been great at small talk, it's not part of my personality and I struggled for years in these types of situations preferring to stay on the outside of the room, only talking to the people I knew.

Since then I've learned that meeting new people can be a lot of fun, especially when you find a group that shares your values and ethics. But if meeting new people or being in unfamiliar situations causes you stress, ask yourself why.

Perhaps like me you struggle with small talk, maybe you don't like how you look or you're worried people will judge you. But in fact people love to talk about themselves. So I've been able to overcome my stress in these situations by asking people about themselves: their lives, their work and their interests. The conversation flows, I feel more comfortable and I'm engaging in conversation and therefore looking and feeling less awkward. I've also learned that I love learning about other people.

Think of a time where you did meet new people and it all worked out well. What caused it to go well? How can you recreate that?

The next time you have to attend an event go with a plan to meet at least one new person or learn one new thing rather than focusing on what you're dreading.

While you are there you could try my Three Ps (find them at the end of this book) and see what a difference they make to your stress levels. You never know, you might even enjoy it!

Everyone else seems to be having a better time than me

When we compare our lives to social media posts, updates and pictures we often worry about our lives being dull and boring in comparison.

But the majority of the social media posts we see are just cleverly curated snapshots.

Celebrities posting images of other people's private planes and luxurious properties, yoga teachers in poses that they can only hold for three seconds and pictures of healthy food which don't show the side order of fries. Fortunately fitness bloggers such as the Bad Yogi exist to present a more realistic picture of fitness[1] and people such as model Rebecca Pearson are speaking out and exposing the reality behind the Photoshopped pictures.[2]

A moment captured on social media doesn't show the reality of the situation

So remember that a moment captured on social media doesn't show the reality of the situation. People don't post what they look like first thing in the morning, or the

---

1   https://www.badyogi.com
2   http://www.telegraph.co.uk/women/womens-life/11980031/
Instagram-confession-The-ugly-truth-behind-my-perfect-model-
shots.html

pile of washing mounting up in the laundry basket, the overgrown garden or the number of emails waiting for a response in their inbox.

People create an image of a perfect life because it makes them feel good about themselves, regardless of whether it shows the reality of their life.

Try to gain some perspective: photos showing two minutes from one day don't show the other twenty three hours and fifty eight minutes.

Also, remember that you have a choice about who and what you let into your life. In short you can ignore or block posts, unfriend or unfollow people or remove yourself from social media entirely. You can choose not to see the posts which make you feel unhappy.

I worry about what people think of me

Not everyone is going to like you, and that's ok. I'm sure you don't like everyone either.

Have you done anything wrong? Have you said anything wrong? What is it that you think people will think or say about you?

If people are talking about you it could be for any number of reasons: jealousy, concern, love or nosiness.

You can't stop people talking about you. Maybe they actually think you are amazing but just haven't got round to telling you or maybe they aren't thinking about you at all because they are focusing on what's going on in their own lives.

I know successful business owners whose family members think they are a failure. I also know senior directors in global organisations whose partners think they could be doing better and parents whose children have achieved some amazing things but whose own parents still think they could have pushed their children further.

We can't change other people's perceptions but we can learn to avoid letting their perceptions impact how we feel.

Get comfortable with yourself and live with integrity: do the right things even when nobody else is looking. Know who you are, what your values are and what's important to you and you'll be less likely to waste energy on worrying about what others may or may not be saying about you. Focus on how *you* feel about yourself.

Get comfortable with yourself and live with integrity

See more about knowing what's important to you in "I find it hard to say no to people".

I get stressed about everything that's going on in the world

The events of recent years have caused all of us to worry more about global and political issues. But how is worrying about it going to change it?

If you are going to worry about everything that happens in the world, you are going to be constantly stressed. Is it sad when terrible things happen? Of course. But you can't live your entire life worrying about these things.

Instead, take action and make a difference where you can in the world, and focus your attention on living your own life with integrity and love. Think of just one difference that you could make at home, in your community or in the wider world. Perhaps it's doing more recycling, helping out an elderly neighbour, car-sharing or volunteering.

Stress, as I've mentioned before, is related to our thought patterns. If you think the world a horrible, awful place, then that is what you will see. Choose to see it differently. Choose to accept that bad things happen in the world and **You can control how you live your own life** that you can't control the actions of others, but at the same time acknowledge that you can control how you live your own life. Focus on being the best you that you can possibly be and on making a positive impact in your world.

I wouldn't want anyone to think I'm lazy

Frantically rushing around telling everyone how stressed and how busy we are seems to have become the latest fashion. We wouldn't want anyone thinking we are lazy! If just the thought of being called lazy is enough to cause you stress you're likely to keep as busy as possible, and so the cycle will continue.

But as I have said elsewhere, busy does not mean productive or efficient, and being so efficient that you're able to create some downtime doesn't mean you're lazy.

I know people who feel guilty if they are actually calm, productive and not stressed. We need to change this way of thinking, and doing and being.

When was the last time you had a productive day? Not a busy day but a productive, efficient day?

I recently spoke to a client who told me how busy they were, and when they asked how I was I replied 'I'm busy' too. Then I stopped and corrected myself:

"Busy, you know with a lot going on but no more than usual. Things are going really well and I am being really productive and making great progress". This changed our perspective. By focusing on being busy, we get more of the feeling of being busy. By focusing on making progress, we make progress.

Even just changing your language and using 'productive' instead of 'busy' can be a great step change. Remember it's your thoughts which impact your stress levels, not the events in your life.

And remember, taking time out to recharge is completely okay. It's not selfish, you don't have to feel guilty. It's essential for you to continue to be able to do what you need to do in life, including the things you most enjoy.

> Taking time out to recharge is completely okay

See also "I'm always first in and last out".

I find it hard to say no to people

If I had a pound for every time I've heard this excuse I would be retired and sunning myself on a beach somewhere exotic right now. I hear it all the time from clients, family and friends.

Many of us don't feel able to just say no. So when we can't think of a reason we just keep saying yes, adding more and more to our to-do lists, filling up our stress buckets by doing all we can to please others.

At times helping others will be the right thing to do, but taking on more and more is not going to do you or anyone else any favours when you collapse in a heap through stress or sheer exhaustion.

I believe that the key to identifying what you should and shouldn't take on is clarity on your own purpose, which is what you want or need to achieve for yourself and feel about yourself.

In his book *Start With Why* Simon Sinek says that it doesn't matter what you do, it only matters why you do it.[3] He discusses leaders like Martin Luther King Jr and Steve Jobs and notes that people like this think in the same way – they start with why. He believes that we should move away from knowing what we do and how we do it to why we do it.

Asking yourself this can help you to identify your own purpose and to know which paths and actions will be most fulfilling for you.

If you can get clearer on this, these questions can then help you to decide whether you should be saying yes or no to requests for help:

---

3   Simon Sinek, *Start With Why: How Great Leaders Inspire Everyone to Take Action, Penguin, 2001*

- Will this help me achieve my purpose?
- Is this a priority right now?

If the answer isn't yes to both of these questions then your answer could be no. That's not to say you can't choose to put loved ones first in some instances, nor that you shouldn't sometimes choose to help people out, but saying yes shouldn't be your default position. If you never put yourself first, you'll suffer in the long run.

One of my clients was struggling to fit in all of the driving that she was doing for her sons and their friends. She found that other parents expected her to be the driver because they were 'too busy' and she was feeling stressed. It was making her unhappy because she felt she couldn't say no, she didn't want to let her sons or the other parents down and was always frantically trying to juggle her own diary to find time for this. She was driving to the school bus during the week, cricket and rugby matches at weekends and parties in the evenings, as well as working full time and keeping up with day-to-day household chores and looking after an elderly neighbour.

She started to say no to these requests. At first she would say she couldn't because she had something else to do and offer an alternative day or time that she could help and then she found she didn't have to give an alternative or an excuse, because the word 'no' can be a complete sentence which works on its own. Responsibilities got shared with other parents, she had more time to herself and even found time to start reading her favourite books again. Her stress levels decreased, she felt more calm and more in control. She still does her share but she no longer shoulders all of the responsibility.

You might also want to read "I don't know how to prioritise" and "Everyone expects so much from me".

I don't feel appreciated

The only person who needs to appreciate what you do and recognise the value in what you do is *you*.

It would of course be nice for other people to demonstrate their appreciation, but most of the time people don't thank you or show appreciation simply because they are focused on their own tasks and plans.

Don't feel guilty about acknowledging your own successes and efforts. Blow your own trumpet once in a while!

Blow your own trumpet once in a while!

Once you start doing this for yourself you won't be so upset by a lack of feedback from others. And when you appreciate yourself you can start appreciating others and you'll find it becomes reciprocal. So many people expect appreciation from their boss, their partner, their children, their parents or their friends and yet never tell any of these people that they appreciate them. What goes around comes around.

Lifestyle

I've lost sight of what really matters

Take a piece of paper and write at the top of the page 'What is important to me?' Then start answering the question. List the things you like to do and how you like to spend your time. What have you done in the past which you no longer do? What have you always wanted to do? Don't force it, don't question anything that comes to mind, just write it down.

Take another piece of paper and write down all of the things you are doing at the moment.

Then against both lists write down how much time you are spending on each item.

This should illustrate where you're spending time on things which don't matter to you or bring you no pleasure, and what you could ideally be doing instead. For example what's important to you might be spending time with family, but you are spending all of your time at work.

If you switch your energy and attention from the things which don't matter to the things which do it will have an instant impact on your stress levels.

A glass or two of wine helps me cope

Psychologically you may feel that a glass or two of an evening is calming you down, but alcohol can affect your sleep and if you don't get enough good quality sleep you'll ultimately end up feeling more stressed, which can then lead to you drinking more. See more about sleep in "I worry too much".

There are other more effective ways to calm down. Go for a walk, go and sit in the garden, read a book, take a bath, watch a funny movie, bake a cake, call your best friend, go for dinner with your partner or do something creative with your kids.

If you want a drink then by all means have a drink but don't do it in the belief that it's calming you down.

I've forgotten how to relax

Do you find that as soon as your head hits the pillow at night you start thinking of things to do, or that ideas come to you or solutions to problems you've been trying to figure out all day so that you then struggle to get to sleep because your mind is whirring? Do you find that you get your best ideas in the shower, or the bathroom?

This is because it's the only time of the day where you allow yourself to hear your thoughts. It's great to have ideas, but if they come at a time when you need to sleep, or when you want some quiet time, or when you're in the shower with no way of writing them down, it can prevent you relaxing.

Ideally you need more thinking time during the day in order to avoid this happening when you are trying to relax. So schedule that into your working day.

Quiet time when your mind can slow down and not buzz with thoughts is vital for your health, your wellbeing and your stress levels. If you're not used to relaxing then it can be a difficult thing to do. I used to assume that relaxing meant doing nothing and because I didn't consider myself a lazy 'do nothing' kind of person I tried to convince myself that doing anything which wasn't work meant I was relaxing. I would cycle, write, read or go out with my other half, my friends or my sons. All of these things helped me to switch off to some extent but it was all doing *something*.

More recently I have changed my approach to relaxation. I learned to journal, which involves writing down my thoughts and feelings about the events of my life. I have also learned to meditate. The journaling gets all of the noise out of my head and the meditation helps me to focus on what's important and guides me toward what to do next. At first this felt awkward, but with practice it became easier and I've done this now for several years. Some friends and clients of mine don't find these practices helpful and prefer instead to be outdoors, have a massage or do yoga. It doesn't matter what you do, but find your own way to clear your head. It may be that just having a shower or bath or laying quietly on your bed is a good way to quieten your mind before you go to sleep, but find something and practise it regularly.

> It doesn't matter what you do, but find your own way to clear your head

Smoking helps me cope

As an ex-smoker I've been there, done that, got the t-shirt. I too told myself that smoking helped to calm me down, but it didn't.

Not one of the four thousand chemicals in tobacco is a relaxant nor do any of them reduce stress. The chemicals are stimulants and will actually make you *more* stressed. Research commissioned by the British

Heart Foundation demonstrated that smokers are seventy percent more likely to suffer from anxiety and depression than non-smokers, as a direct result of their smoking.[4]

So you might want to consider giving up in order to improve your current and future health, both physical and mental. Better health will make you more resilient and more able to deal with stress.

Better health will make you more resilient and more able to deal with stress.

Now, we're led to believe that smoking is highly addictive. Pharmaceutical companies want you to believe that nicotine is physically addictive because that means you need to buy substitutes such as gum from them in order to kick the habit.

However I believe that smoking is more of a habit than a chemical addiction.[5] Knowing that doesn't make it any easier to stop, but remember you go all through the night without a cigarette and you can sit through a movie at the cinema, a meeting at work or a long flight without a cigarette too.

---

4   http://www.dailymail.co.uk/health/article-2965408/Why-s-no-thing-calming-cigarette-Smokers-70-suffer-anxiety-depression-quitting-reverse-damage.html
5   See http://www.scientificpsychic.com/health/smoking-psychology.html for a list of reasons people might smoke out of habit

The half-life of nicotine is remarkably short: only one or two hours, so you actually experience the most significant withdrawal symptoms very soon after stubbing out your last cigarette.[6] That's the worst it gets!

Smoking does not help you cope with stress. If you give it up you can expect more energy, a feeling of calm and more money in the bank. You'll breathe easier, you'll smell nicer and your friends and family will be pleased.

See also "A glass or two of wine helps me cope" for ideas on activities which really will help you calm down.

I don't have the time or energy to look after myself

Exercise make us feel calmer: it gets our blood pumping, our happy hormones flowing and helps to clear our heads. Eating healthily also makes us better able to cope with life's pressures.

Life is easier when we're fit, well-nourished and physically resilient. However exercise and eating well are often the first

Life is easier when we're fit, well-nourished and physically resilient

---

6   http://science.howstuffworks.com/nicotine1.htm

things to be neglected when we're short of time.

On a leadership course a few years ago I learned an exercise which I still do daily. It's called EARN.[7]

Here's how to do it:

At the end of a day, write down the letters E, A, R and N on a piece of paper and give yourself a score of 0 to 5 for the day:

E = Exercise

Did you run, walk, do yoga, cycle, swim, walk the dog, take the stairs instead of the lift? Anything that got you moving

A = Attitude

How did you feel throughout the day? Were you negative or were you able to see the bright side of things? Were you happy, angry, stressed, irritated, did you worry?

R = Rejuvenation

What did you do to relax? Did you go for a walk, meditate, read a book, listen to music, paint, cook, have a long soak in a bath?

---

7   *Tribal Leadership course, http://www.culturesync.net/*

N = Nutrition

How did you fuel your body? Did you make healthy choices to make you feel energised or did you choose foods which made you feel sluggish and lethargic?

You shouldn't feel bad if you don't score a 5 in all areas, this exercise is designed to help you to think about how you've nurtured yourself throughout the day in order to make better choices tomorrow.

You'll probably find patterns in your behaviour. For example, if I exercise in the morning I'm likely to make better food choices throughout the day which will make me feel better and make me want to write in my journal or meditate in the evening.

If I wake up in a bad mood I am probably less likely to exercise so I'll eat unhealthy foods throughout the day which will impact my mood and I may spend the evening watching rubbish TV and then be unable to sleep well.

You only need a small amount of time to fit in some exercise

So if you make small improvements in one area you may automatically improve in others.

You only need a small amount of time to fit in some exercise and it doesn't have to involve a trip to the gym, especially if that doesn't motivate or interest you. Yoga can take fifteen minutes if you follow the right routine, a run can be done in thirty minutes. Check out YouTube for fifteen minute intense workouts which you can do at home and search for apps which offer similar ideas. Build activity into your life: take the stairs instead of the lift, get a dog if you haven't already or borrow one and take it for a walk. If you've got kids take them to the park and do some cartwheels or handstands with them or if you've got a baby walk or run with the pushchair up a hill.

In terms of healthy eating, if you're standing in your kitchen exhausted by a day's work and too tired to think about creating a healthy meal, you don't automatically have to reach for something unhealthy. Some vegetable soup, scrambled eggs or a slice of wholemeal toast with peanut butter followed by a piece of fruit would be better than, say, a packet of biscuits or a pizza delivery and would take only a few minutes to prepare. And try to plan in advance so that you always have some healthy options available, possibly prepared weekly and stored in the freezer. Also, keep some healthy snacks in your bag or desk drawer so that you have something healthy to hand at all times.

Try some of these ideas and you'll become aware of how exercise and better nutrition can increase your energy, make you feel better about yourself and decrease your stress.

See also the Three Ps at the end of this book – positive actions, positive interactions and positive thoughts. Everything we do in a day has a knock-on effect on how we feel and we can choose whether that effect is good or not.

Finally, you might like to take a look at two other books in this series, What's Your Excuse for not Getting Fit? and What's Your Excuse for not Eating Healthily? by Joanne Henson, which offer much more advice on how to take better care of yourself.[8]

---

8   Joanne Henson, What's Your Excuse for not Getting Fit? and What's Your Excuse for not Eating Healthily? WYE Publishing, 2015

Organisation

I don't know how to prioritise

There are countless books and training courses which claim to help you to effectively manage your time and to-do lists but I find that many people struggle to put these systems into practice.

I believe that's because the key to effective prioritisation is being clear on what you want to achieve and what's important to you and until you are clear on that you will find it hard to know what needs to be tackled first.

In his book Start With Why Simon Sinek says, 'People don't buy what you do; they buy why you do it. And what you do simply proves what you believe'.[9] Consider this in relation to your own life to help you to identify what is most important to you.

I've also written about this in my own book Create Your Purpose, Manage Your Time. I wrote the book to help people to understand how by living with purpose you can more effectively manage your time.[10]

---

9   Simon Sinek, Start With Why: How Great Leaders Inspire Everyone to Take Action, Penguin, 2001
10   Kelly Swingler, Create Your Purpose, Manage Your Time, Amazon Kindle, 2014

A business owner I know has an ever growing to-do list. She refers to it daily and every day she adds things to it. Just looking at it makes her stressed because she never gets to the bottom of it. This is because most of the tasks are of no value to her or her business, but because they are on the list she feels she needs to do them anyway. Her stress would be reduced if she were able to recognise this, but instead she struggles on.

If you have a similar approach to your to-do list, try this:

- Ask yourself, 'Is this a priority right now and will this help me achieve my purpose?'
- Schedule the things you need to get done in your diary
- Write down any ideas that occur to you throughout the week separately and review them every Friday: what's important goes on the to-do list, what was just a crazy idea goes in the bin

Don't let your to-do list control you. Use it as a tool to manage your time effectively and to evaluate what matters rather than what will simply be a source of stress.

Don't let your to-do list control you

You might also want to read "I find it hard to say

no to people" and "I have too much to do" for more on using your vision or purpose to help with priorities.

The morning routine is a nightmare

I assume you have kids! I know, it can be a nightmare and I applaud you on your patience and perseverance. (It does get easier over time, I promise!)

You wake up and instantly switch into stressed mode: you can't find your clothes, you get shampoo in your eyes in the shower, you almost slip when you rush down the stairs, you spill your coffee down your shirt, your kids spill cereal and milk in the chaos at the table, you're unable to find your car keys and searching for them makes you late. When you get into the car the traffic is terrible and you arrive late for your first meeting. Now your whole day is going to be one big fat stressful mess.

Let's try that again.

You wake up feeling calm. Your clothes are hanging up on the outside of the wardrobe where you left them last night, you enjoy you shower, get dressed, wake the kids on your way downstairs and ask them to help with breakfast. You make your coffee, get everyone ready and on the way out you pick up your keys from their usual place. The traffic always starts to improve as soon as you drop off the kids but you've got plenty of time, you arrive at the office with ten minutes to spare so you grab another coffee and head off to your meeting. Today is going to be a good day.

How do you switch from the first scenario to the second?

Create a routine, a better routine.

Prepare things the night before. Make a note and leave it on the fridge or stuck to the front door if you need to remember things. Make sure everyone is in bed the night before at a decent time, and allow no tech or stimulants during the two hours before bed.

In the morning ensure that everyone is up early enough to have time to do what they need to do and then leave the house with plenty of time for the journey.

Delegate what you can to the kids and your partner

Don't do everything yourself, delegate what you can to the kids and your partner.

This will take time and you'll need to work at it, but if you make gradual small improvements and stick with them a calmer, less stressful morning routine will take shape. And the result of a calm morning is a calmer day.

I never seem to achieve anything

It can be really easy to spend all of your time focusing on an end goal and feeling stressed or overwhelmed by everything you need to do to get there.

I was going on a holiday with some friends a while ago and had to drive two hundred miles to get there. This was going to be the furthest I had ever driven on my own and the longest journey I had taken since being diagnosed with epilepsy. I was very stressed about the thought of two hundred miles in the car.

I set off but after forty-eight miles I was so stressed I couldn't breathe. I pulled over and calmed myself down. I gave myself a talking to, took some deep breaths and set off again. This time I only focused on the next twenty miles and after that the next twenty. That's all I did all the way there and all the way back. The overall goal felt too difficult for me, but taking it in smaller steps felt manageable.

Apply this approach to your own goal. Work out the steps you need to take to get there, even if it's a list of lots of tiny steps, and then focus on just one of those steps at a time. Then once you've reached one milestone, move on to the next.

Take one step at a time, and you'll be much less likely to get stuck due to stress.

Social Life

I don't want to miss out on anything

FOMO – Fear of Missing Out – is on the increase, largely due to how much time we spend fixating on the lives of others through the lens of social media. We want to have equally interesting lives!

Aside from social media, we don't want to say no to dinner with friends, weekends away or days out because we fear we might miss out on something great. So we squeeze yet another event into our schedules, get stressed because we don't have time to prepare and then possibly even get stressed when we are there because we may feel we should be elsewhere or doing something else.

A friend of mine was stressed recently because she had four trips over four different weekends with family and friends and she was worried she wouldn't have time to pack, wouldn't have time to fit in her washing and ironing, wouldn't be able to switch off from work and wouldn't know what her family were doing on the weekends she was away from them. Yet she had *agreed* to four consecutive weekends because she didn't want to miss out on anything.

There will be times when you can't make something or when saying yes to another invitation will overload you, and in those cases you should just send your apologies and best wishes and focus on where you are and who you are with. There will be other dinners, other invitations and other events.

There's another aspect to this too. Technology now allows us to mentally be in more than one place at once. I went away with another friend of mine recently. She couldn't tear herself away from her phone: texts, calls, Facebook, Twitter, emails. I showed her a meme: 'Spend time with people who make you forget your phone'. She apologized but explained that she felt the need to be in constant contact with the many people in her life because she doesn't want to miss out on anything. Even though this means she's never actually fully present in the moment. She misses out on what she should be enjoying there and then and her mind is constantly multi-tasking.

> There will be other dinners, other invitations and other events

If this resonates with you, consider how this is putting you under additional stress. Instead of focusing on what other people are doing elsewhere, pay attention to what is going on around you in the here and now. Stay present. It's much less stressful.

I can't remember the last time I went out with friends

If spending time with friends is important to you then treat it as a priority. I hear so many people talking about waiting until they have the time before they can make things happen. Well guess what? Time doesn't magically appear in your schedule unless you create it.

That's right, you need to *create* the time.

That means making the effort to find some space, and using it to create a social life. Sitting and waiting, letting other things take over and looking back in six months' time regretting what you haven't done won't make you happy.

I have learned to create space for my social life as I know that a healthy social life is good for my stress levels. I book a weekend away with one group of friends twice a year, and nights out with other friends once a month or fortnight. Sometimes it's a get-together with a big group at one of our houses and we get the kids involved so that it's not a case of sacrificing one relationship for another.

Schedule meetings well in advance, set dates and stick to them. Enjoy looking forward to them.

It's important to remember that as we get older and have our own families our friendships can take a bit of a back seat. It's not necessarily something to be concerned about, it's just normal life. Planning will become more important but it is possible to find time to enjoy and nurture your friendships. And the pleasure you get from those times will leave you refreshed and more able to deal with the more stressful times in your life.

I can't remember the last time I did something I really enjoyed

Perhaps you are at a stage in your life when other, similarly enjoyable things have taken over? As we grow and as our lives change what we used to enjoy may no longer serve us, or may get replaced by other activities. So consider whether you're missing something you used to do but not appreciating new things in your life.

But if you've stopped doing what you enjoy because you no longer feel you have the time to fit it in, be proactive and create the time for it. Schedule a date with yourself. See "I can't remember the last time I went out with friends" above for more on how to do this.

Anticipation

I always seem to have too much to do

Do you get stressed just thinking about it?

Sometimes the thinking can be worse than the actual doing and delaying action can at times make it more stressful. Overthinking things can also be stressful if you start to imagine all of the different scenarios which could happen.

If the thought of taking action is making you unhappy, try to identify why. I've found over the years that when people worry about taking action it can be because they doubt their own abilities, or have a fear of failure, or even a fear of success. The key is to take the first step, to create positive thoughts surrounding your own abilities, perhaps with some *I am* statements and to go for it.

I am statements or affirmations are something I use daily, for example:

I am calm
I am happy
I am productive

I am successful
I am able

You could also try to:

- Focus on one thing at a time. By doing so you will get each task completed more quickly and you'll be making progress which will allow you to start to feel more in control
- Let go of the unnecessary things from the list. Some things that once felt like a priority might not be any longer. Consider what you need to do and let go of what you don't need to do
- Be clear on the timelines in which you need to get everything done. By the end of the day isn't always a helpful timeline. Be specific about the exact time
- Delegate. Let go of some things on your list and delegate to someone who can help or even someone who could do it quicker and better than you
- Stop thinking and take action instead. Overthinking won't help you get things done and if you are procrastinating, go back to the procrastinating chapter

It's easy to fall into the trap of thinking you have too much to do but if you follow the steps above you'll soon start to notice the difference in your thoughts and you'll be able to take some first steps so that you become more effective and much less stressed.

I'm dreading a difficult conversation

So you're avoiding it? If you do that the person or people you need to speak to will never get to hear what you have to say and therefore won't be in a position to take any action or change anything to make things easier for you.

It's also not good for you because you're holding onto all of the stuff that you should be saying. The more you hold onto it the more stress you'll experience and you'll be even less likely to initiate the conversation.

So putting off the conversation isn't easier. Having the conversation is actually the best option, because when you've had the conversation you can let go of all of the related tension.

Here's how to have that conversation. I call it HOT: Honest, Open, Transparent:

- Name the issue or topic of the conversation
- Describe a specific example that illustrates the

behaviour or situation you want to change or a decision that has already been made

* Describe how the issue is making you feel
* Clarify what's at stake. If the decision or change isn't made what's going to happen?
* Admit your contribution to the problem. Nobody is blameless and this helps to minimise conflict
* Indicate your wish to resolve the issue
* Invite the other person to respond

Give this a go the next time you need to have a difficult conversation. The first few times may feel a little daunting, but you'll get used to it quite quickly and when you experience how good it feels to let go of bottled up feelings you'll be much more likely to tackle future conversations in the same way.

I worry about tackling new things

Are you stressed to the point of not being able to take action? What if you weren't stressed but excited by it?

Can you swap the word 'stressed' for the word 'excited'?

Physiologically, there's not much of a difference

between the two. Your heart rate increases, your breathing becomes shallow, you may get a strange feeling in your stomach. The only difference is how you play it out in your head.

Give it a go, 'I am excited'.

Ifs and Whens

I'll be less stressed when the kids start school

I thought this too, but unless you only work from 9:30 to 3:00 or you run your own business, this won't be the case.

They won't be allowed at school if they have even the slightest stomach upset. They will catch colds and bugs. The school will close in bad weather, teacher training days will clash with important meetings, you'll have assemblies, plays, performances and sports days to attend and childcare issues during the frequent holidays.

So unfortunately you can't look forward to a reduction in stress as soon as your kids are old enough for school, and you should take steps to tackle your stress now.

From my own experience and from talking to other mums, it can be the perception of what the perfect family should look like that can cause us stress. You want to keep your house tidy, you've got work to do, meals to cook, washing to do. You want quality, fun time with the kids but housework or other responsibilities come first and then you beat yourself up because everyone else seems to be managing perfectly.

What can you let go of today that will make a difference? Can the washing-up wait until tonight or tomorrow morning? Can someone else help you for an hour? Identity your priorities, take note of what's important and what isn't.

Looking ahead to when the kids do start school, get key dates in advance from the school so that you can plan accordingly. Find other mums that you can buddy up with on unplanned school closure days and take it in turns to help each other. Plan alternate days off with your partner so that you each do your fair share. Have a conversation in advance with your boss about how things can be made to work and explain you may need a bit more flexibility. Put plans in place now for a smooth transition into the next phase of your kids' lives.

I'll be less stressed when the kids finish their exams

After exams comes the waiting for the grades then more school, or college or university and all of the added pressures that come with this. You'll worry about whether they are working hard enough, whether they will get the grades, whether they will find a job. You'll be upset if they don't get the grades because you'll wonder what's next for them and when they do get interviews you'll worry about them. So deal with your stress now, it isn't going to go away!

Schedule some time to help them with their revision, but plan fun days and days off too. Just as

Deal with your stress now, it isn't going to go away!

we should create quiet time for ourselves, the same is true for our kids: they need mental time out too.

Also, talk to your kids about Plan A and Plan B. Don't make it your plan – it's their life and they need to live it their way – but provide a safety blanket for them. Talk about alternatives, different routes and when you see them feeling comfortable with the situation you'll feel better too.

I'll be less stressed when the kids leave home

I'm currently waiting for that day to come. The end of piles of clothes on bedroom floors, dishes in the sink, lending money, last minute washing and ironing, searches for lost items and lifts in the car because they are running late. And at times I do feel stressed about it, but I'll miss the day it no longer happens. Kids grow fast, so I'm learning to appreciate the trail of mess they leave behind them as a reminder that they are still at home.

Identify what the stress is now and why you think it will be easier when they leave home. Is it the pile of clothes, the lack of sleep as you wait up for them to come home after a night out, or something else? Tackle this now so that you can enjoy the time you have with your kids before they leave home.

Enjoy the time you have with your kids before they leave home

And then create a plan for the future so that you have exciting things to fill your life when they've gone. You'll miss them.

I'll be less stressed when we've moved house

Yes you probably will be, but that's no excuse not to tackle the stress you're going through now if it is making you unhappy and affecting your health.

Admittedly, moving house can be stressful and if you are in a chain and waiting on other people the lack of control over the situation can start to take its toll. So what can you do to make things easier?

First, accept that things will take time and that you probably can't do very much about that. Acceptance will go a long way to helping you cope when you don't have control of the situation.

Then focus on what you can control:

- Declutter now by getting rid of what you don't need to take to the new house, give items a new home with someone else
- Make an early start on packing and don't leave it to the last minute
- Make a checklist of the administrative tasks in advance: cancelling or transferring services, redirecting your post, etc

And, when you've moved, accept you may have to live with boxes for a while. Take your time and put things in the right place so that your new home feels like a home instead of a car boot sale.

There will come a time when the upheaval will be over and you can then enjoy your new surroundings and enjoy the resulting reduction in stress levels.

I'll be less stressed after the wedding

A wedding is a wonderful event, but the marriage is more important.

The planning doesn't have to be stressful. Make a plan, know what you want and stick to it. Don't get sucked into bright shiny object syndrome where you feel you have to have so many table decorations and favours that there isn't actually any room for food on the table. Spending money you may not have on things you don't need is something you can do without.

Invite who you want to invite, keep things simple and if you're worried that two people are going to ruin the day because they haven't spoken to each other in years, have a word with them well in advance, explain how important the day is for you and give them consequences about what will happen if they let their own bickering ruin your big day. I know people who have cancelled their wedding and eloped because divorced parents were too busy squabbling to put the happiness of their child first.

Do what you want. It's your day

And don't bother trying to outdo your best friend's wedding or trying to make your wedding the best wedding in the world.

Focus on what the day means to you and it will be *your* best wedding ever.

Do what you want. It's *your* day. Where's the stress in that?

I'd be less stressed if I had more money

When money is tight it can be a major cause of stress, and if you are in debt it can make the situation even worse.

But there are some things you can do to help yourself.

Can you stop buying a morning coffee from the coffee shop around the corner? Can you transfer your credit card debt to a different provider and reduce the interest? Do you have anything you can sell? Or can you reduce some of your expenditure elsewhere?

The BBC recently broadcast a series called Eat Well for Less. In the series they demonstrated how by moving from branded goods to own brand products you can make significant savings. Just because you've always used the most expensive face cream, toothpaste or perfume doesn't mean you have to continue doing so. You don't always need the expensive car or expensive clothes to look or feel good.

Convenience foods can be much more expensive

than cooking from scratch so you could invest a little more time and save a lot of money by looking at the way you eat.

Choose camping over an all-inclusive holiday abroad, change energy provider, shop at places that give cash back or vouchers.

And look for ways to earn more money, such as selling some items that you don't need on eBay.

A coaching client of mine recently came to a session and said that she was going to have to stop working with me as she could no longer afford it. We talked it through, and within three weeks she had found the means to continue coaching but more importantly to book herself a holiday, just by taking stock of her expenditure and taking action to reduce it.

Finally, don't focus on what you *don't* have. Instead spend time thinking about all of the good things that do you have in your life for which you can be grateful.

I'd be less stressed if I won the lottery

Money can have a big impact on our lives. Not having enough money can be hard if you're worrying about where the next meal is going to come from or whether or not you can keep a roof over your head.

If you're tolerating stress over money issues because you're hoping for a big win, you'll be stressed forever. I've just googled the chances of winning the lottery, and you have a 1 in 14 million chance of winning, or to be exact, 1 in 13,983,816.[11]

So let this dream go. Be brave and take stock of your finances. Find a different way to make money and live the life you want.

Having money can also bring stress. It can put pressure on relationships and leave people focusing on the material things in life instead of focusing on the important things.

Having money can also bring stress

So please do not avoid taking action about financial worries by hankering after something which is very, very unlikely to happen. Focus on what you do have control over.

You might find that one of the other books in this series, What's Your Excuse for not Being Better With Money? by Jo Thresher, can help you to take control of your finances and improve your relationship with money.[12]

---

11 http://lottery.merseyworld.com/Info/Chances.html
12 Jo Thresher, What's Your Excuse for not Being Better With Money? WYE Publishing, 2017

I'd be less stressed if I had a cleaner

If household chores are making you unhappy, are you spreading the load fairly with other members of your household? You don't have to do everything yourself.

But actually, what's stopping you getting a cleaner? Yes, there's a cost, but it might well be worth it. What could you give up or reduce to find the money? Even if you can only afford an hour a week or a monthly visit it's work you wouldn't have to do.

Getting a cleaner was the best thing I ever did. Spending the weekend elbow deep in cleaning products was not my idea of fun, especially when I'd spent all week working my backside off.

It might feel like a luxury but if it saves you time and allows you to put your feet up and relax then actually what you're doing is investing in your long-term health.

I'd be less stressed if I could lose weight

If this relates to worrying about what people think of you, why do you care? Let it go. It won't matter if people think you are too fat, or too thin, or just right, if you're not happy with yourself then your size isn't going to make you happy.

Small minded, judgmental people will judge you whatever your size and weight because putting others down makes them feel better. I recently watched a group of women on TV criticising another woman for being too thin. I thought she looked good and that she looked healthy. I thought it obvious by the way they spoke about themselves that they were simply envious.

So stop worrying about what other people think of you – see "I worry about what people think of me" for advice on how to do this.

If you are unhappy about your weight, take action to do something about it. Take it slowly, make some gradual changes. It can be done and when you're a healthier weight and feeling better about yourself you'll feel less stressed, more calm and much more in control.

> Don't put your life on hold – fun now will be good for you

In the meantime don't put your life on hold – fun now will be good for you and including some pleasure in your life will reduce your current feelings of stress and unhappiness. Don't wait until everything is perfect!

Some Final Thoughts

Stress isn't something that is forced upon us. Stress is our reaction to a situation or to other people's actions. Just as nobody can make us feel angry, sad, happy, etc without out compliance, nothing and nobody can actually *make* us feel stressed. It's our actions, our thoughts and our interactions which dictate our stress levels and it's how we handle the events, situations and relationships in our lives that matters.

Nothing and nobody can actually *make* us feel stressed

Remember that not all stress is bad. A healthy amount of stress is what gets us out of bed each day. It helps us to meet deadlines and achieve success in our lives. But if the stress in your life is overwhelming you need to address it for the good of your mental and physical health.

You've now read my advice on how you can change the way you handle events and manage your stress levels, and I hope that you've found some useful ideas to put into practice.

Here are the key things I hope you've noted, and which will make a real difference to how you feel about your life, plus a few other ideas to help you move on to a calmer, happier life:

Improve Your Sleep

I believe that the biggest cause of stress in our lives is a lack of sleep. When we don't sleep we start to make poor choices with our food and drink, we withdraw from the things that make us feel good about ourselves, we start to doubt ourselves and then we find ourselves in a downward spiral of unhappiness.

So if you only do one thing for yourself after reading this book, improve your sleep.

Eat Healthier Foods

Eating healthily means you will have more energy, fewer energy dips during the day and improved sleep. When you eat foods that make you feel sluggish you are more likely to procrastinate, not know where to start and let things start to pile up and overwhelm you. And reaching for sugar or caffeine for a quick fix won't help with your sleep or your stress levels.

Try to minimise processed, refined and sugary foods and caffeinated drinks and instead opt for natural, whole foods and lots of fresh fruit and vegetables which will nourish you and improve your energy levels.

Spend Time Outside

The more time you can spend outside the better. Maybe swap a train journey for a walk or your car for a bike, or just take a walk at lunchtime or in the evenings. Being outside not only provides us with fresh air, but being closer to nature makes us feel better about ourselves. Health journalist Chloe Metzger says that spending time outside can ease depression, improve our outlook, improve our focus and increase our immunity.[13] What's not to love about that?

Get it all out of your head

Get all of the noise out of your head in whatever way works for you. When we're feeling overwhelmed it can be hard to think clearly or to know where to start with something or what our priorities are. This can make things feel more

Find *your* way of emptying your mind

stressful than they actually are. My partner likes to write lists. I prefer writing in a journal, yoga and meditation. My mum practises mindfulness.[14] A friend of mine

13   http://www.health.com/mind-body/health-benefits-of-nature
14   Find out more about mindfulness at http://franticworld.com/what-is-mindfulness/

dictates her to-do list into her phone. Find *your* way of emptying your mind so that you can think more clearly and don't feel so overwhelmed.

Create 'me time'

Time for yourself is so important, but don't wait for time to present itself; create time. It might be fifteen minutes a day, one day every month or an afternoon each week. Take the time and do something you enjoy. Start the book you always wanted to write (if Liz Gilbert can do it in fifteen minutes a day so can you[15]), run, read, paint, dance, listen to music, go for a drive, go to the gym, soak in a bath, watch your favourite film or go to see some art. This is *your* time.

And before you start thinking to yourself that this would be really selfish. It's not! If you don't take time for yourself, how will you keep finding the time and the energy to look after everyone else? On a crashing plane you have to put your own oxygen on first.

Listen to the language you are using

'I'm so stressed' is likely to keep you stressed. Perhaps you are overworked, tired, emotional, unable to

---

15   Liz Gilbert, *Big Magic*, Riverhead Books, 2015

prioritise, short of time or in need of help. Really drill down into how you are feeling before you go painting yourself with the stress brush. The closer you can get to expressing how you are really feeling, the closer you are to finding the best solution.

Understand your why and prioritise accordingly

Understand what your *why* is: what drives you and why it's important to you. Once you understand this you can let go of anything which doesn't align with this. Prioritise in all areas of your life: know what you need to do and by when you need to do it. If it's not important, don't worry about it now, or at all.

You might also want to practise the Three Ps – Positive actions, Positive interactions, Positive thoughts – which I use in my one-to-one work with my coaching clients and which are a helpful framework in which to make meaningful change:

Positive actions
What we do and how we behave

For example, procrastination is an action; so too is getting on with a task. Sitting watching TV is an action as is taking the dog for a walk. Everything we do during the day is an action and if we want to overcome stress and introduce more calm into our lives then we need to understand what are positive actions and what aren't and then increase the amount of positive action and reduce the negative.

So if your health is suffering due to a lack of exercise, and it's making you less able to cope with the stress in your life, then take a positive action to make a change. Equally, if your work, or your boss, or any other area of your life is causing you an unhealthy amount of stress, then find a positive action that will make you feel good about yourself and help to reduce your stress levels.

Taking positive actions instead of negative ones, or instead of no action at all, will improve the way you feel about yourself and your life.

Positive interactions
Time with family and friends, great conversations

Our relationships and our interactions can have an enormous impact on our lives and our stress levels. Motivational speaker Jim Rohn said that we become the average of the five people with whom we spend most of our time.[16]

---

16   *https://www.jimrohn.com/*

Over the years I've felt the energy of the people in my life influence my work and my speaking engagements and I can categorise people as energy angels and energy vampires. Angels are the people in your life that fill you with energy, make you feel good, inspire you and are who you want to spend your time with: they are positive, they are who you love spending time with. The vampires have the opposite effect: they drain you of energy, you don't look forward to seeing them, you can't wait to get away from them and they talk negatively about themselves and others.

Of course you can't completely control who you have in your life, but on average, you should aim for a ratio of at least three angels to every one vampire.

Positive thoughts
Creating your own reality

As I've already acknowledged, changing the way you think can at first be a challenge. I'm not saying that you need to be constantly dreaming of rainbows and flowers – life happens and sometimes you can't help but feel low or negative – but it's important to increase your awareness of your own thoughts and what has triggered them, and then work on turning them into something positive.

For example, constantly thinking about being busy

is a negative thought, whereas focusing on being productive is a positive thought. Focusing on being overweight is a negative thought, focusing on being healthy is positive.

It's all a matter of mindset and perspective. Practise replacing negative reactions with more positive ones and notice how much better it makes you feel.

Use these Three Ps to help you to make changes, to readjust your beliefs and to free yourself from self-imposed labels in order to create new and positive ones for yourself. When you do this your worries will decrease and so will your stress levels. You'll be using your energy in a positive way to change the things in your life over which you do have control.

Take action *now*.

Don't wait for your situation to change and hope that the stress will just disappear. Remember, it's our thought patterns which create the stress. If you are stressed now, put some of the ideas in this book into practice *now*. I promise you that the effort you put in to this will pay dividends, and result in a calmer, happier, more fulfilling life as well as giving you more control over the events in your life and more resilience to deal with things in the future. Your future self will thank you for it.

Acknowledgements

Firstly I would like to thank Jo Thresher for connecting me with Joanne Henson, creator of the WYE series. Without you this book would not have been possible.

Thanks to Joanne Henson for the great advice, suggestions and edits, for making the process as painless as possible and for bringing the subject to life.

Thanks to my angels and growing network of amazing women (and men) who drive me, challenge me and believe in me in all areas of my work and life.

Thanks to the Bourikes for the fun, laughter, beer and greek salad. You are always there when I need you and are part of my extended family.

Thanks to my Mum and Dad, my brothers and my sister for their continued support and to my sons for not having a clue what I do but for being proud of me anyway.

And to Mick, my rock, my sounding board, my reality checker and my de-stressor.

About the Author

Kelly Swingler is an award-winning people and change expert who specialises in helping individuals and organisations to do things differently for improved performance.

A qualified executive coach, psychologist, hypnotherapist and psychotherapist with a twenty year career in human resources, organisational development and learning and development, she is passionate about developing others. Through her company Chrysalis Consulting she helps people to reach their full potential by challenging their mindset, actions and patterns of behaviour.

Kelly's personal aim is to help create better workplaces by getting people to love what they do. Kelly and her team want you to explore new ways of doing, being and thinking so that you can be more confident and more in control.

Find out more at:

www.chrysalis-consulting.co.uk

Email: kelly@chrysalis-consulting.co.uk

Twitter: @kelly_swingler

Index

Also in this series

What's Your Excuse for not Being More Productive?

Juliet Landau-Pope
Overcome your excuses, stop procrastinating, get things done

Do you struggle to organise your time? Do you spend too much time planning and not enough time doing? Or are you simply unable to get started with things? Then this is the book for you.

Professional organiser Juliet-Landau Pope takes a look at all of the things you might be telling yourself to explain why you're not being as productive as you'd like, and offers practical advice, ideas and inspiration to help you move forward.

Don't know where to start? Don't have the time? Or do you simply feel overwhelmed? This supportive and motivational book will help you to tackle all of those beliefs and many more so that you can use your time more effectively in order to *get things done*.

Paperback – ISBN 978-0-9956052-2-0
e-book – ISBN 978-0-9956052-3-7

Also in this series

What's Your Excuse for not Eating Healthily?

Joanne Henson
Overcome your excuses and eat well to look good and feel great

Do you wish you could eat more healthily and improve the way you look and feel, but find that all too often life gets in the way? Do you regularly embark on healthy eating plans or diets but find that you just can't stick with them? Then this is the book for you.

This isn't another diet book. Instead it's a look at the things which have tripped you up in the past and offers advice, ideas and inspiration to help you overcome those things this time around.

No willpower? Hate healthy food? Got no time to cook? Crave sugary snacks? Overcome all of these excuses and many more. Change your eating habits and relationship with food *for good*.

Paperback – ISBN 978-0-9933388-2-3
e-book – ISBN 978-0-9933388-3-0

Also in this series

What's Your Excuse for not Being Better With Money?

Jo Thresher
Overcome your excuses and get to grips with your
personal finances

Do you wish you could be savvier with money but find it too daunting? Do you wish you were more in control of your finances but find yourself avoiding taking action? Then this is the book for you.

Personal finance expert Jo Thresher takes a look at all of the reasons you might give for not getting to grips with your money, and offers advice, ideas and inspiration to help you change that.

No time to get organised? Scared to look at your bank statement? Think you're a shopaholic? Not money minded? Overcome all of these excuses and many more. Improve your relationship with your cash and feel more secure, more relaxed and more in control.

Paperback – ISBN 978-0-9956052-0-6
e-book – ISBN 978-0-9956052-1-3

Also in this series

What's Your Excuse for not Living a Life You Love?

Monica Castenetto
Overcome your excuses and lead a happier, more fulfilling life

Are you stuck in a life you don't love? Have you reached a point where your life doesn't feel right for you anymore? Then this book is for you.

This is not yet another self-help book claiming to reveal the secret to permanent happiness. Instead, it helps you to tackle the things which have been holding you back and gives ideas, advice and inspiration to help you move on to a better life.

Don't know what you want? Scared of failure? Hate change? Worried about what others might think? This book will help you overcome all of your excuses and give you the motivation you need to change your life.

Paperback – ISBN 978-0-9933388-4-7
e-book – ISBN 978-0-9933388-5-4

Also in this series

What's Your Excuse for not Loving Your Job?

Amanda Cullen
Overcome your excuses and change the way you feel about your work

Do you have a job which you're not enjoying as much as you know you should? Do you dread Mondays, spend your free time worrying about your work or feel undervalued by your boss or colleagues? If so, this book is for you.

In this supportive and motivational book Amanda Cullen takes a look at the wide variety of excuses we use which keep us stuck and unhappy in our work. She offers ideas and advice on how to tackle issues so that you can take control, make the necessary changes and transform your working life.

Don't like your colleagues? Spend too long in the office? Not confident in your skills? Or just plain bored? Overcome all of these and many more, and learn how to love your job.

Paperback – ISBN 978-0-9933388-6-1
e-book – ISBN 978-0-9933388-7-8

Also in this series

What's Your Excuse for not Getting Fit?

Joanne Henson
Overcome your excuses and get active, healthy and happy

Do you want to be fit, lean and healthy, but find that all too often life gets in the way? Do you own a gym membership you don't use, or take up running every January only to give up in February? Then this is the book for you.

This is not yet another get-fit-quick program. It's a look at the things which have prevented you in the past from becoming the fit, active person you've always wanted to be, and a source of advice, inspiration and ideas to help you overcome those things this time around. Change your habits and attitude to exercise for good.

Too tired? Lacking motivation? Bored by exercise? You won't be after reading this book!

Paperback – ISBN 978-0-9933388-0-9
e-book – ISBN 978-0-9933388-1-6

Also in this series

What's Your Excuse for not Being More Confident?

Charlotta Hughes
Overcome your excuses, increase your confidence, unleash your potential

Do you feel you could achieve much more in life if only you had more confidence? Do you know you'd be happier if you were braver, or had more self-belief? Then this is the book for you.

In this supportive and motivational book former Life Coach of the Year Charlotta Hughes takes a look at all of the ways in which we hold ourselves back and avoid expanding our horizons and she offers advice, ideas and inspiration to help change things.

Scared of failure? Feel unappreciated? Hate change? Worried about what others might think? This book will help you overcome all of your excuses and give you the motivation you need to change the way you feel about yourself.

Paperback – ISBN 978-0-9933388-8-5
e-book – ISBN 978-0-9933388-9-2

Also in this series

What's Your Excuse for not Clearing Your Clutter?

Juliet Landau-Pope
Overcome your excuses, simplify your life, make space for what matters

Do you struggle with clutter in your life? Do you feel overwhelmed by "stuff", feel that you have no space to work on new projects, or feel unable to relax? Then this is the book for you.

Professional organiser Juliet-Landau Pope takes a look at all of the things you tell yourself to explain why you're not able to clear clutter from your life and why it keeps you stuck. She offers advice, ideas and inspiration to help you change that.

Don't know where to start? Too attached to things? Don't like change? Overcome all of these excuses and many more. Tidy up your life, feel calmer and more organised and make space for new projects and experiences.

Paperback – ISBN 978-0-9956052-4-4
e-book – ISBN 978-0-9956052-5-1